ALICE IN THE BADLANDS

Julie Marie Myatt

BROADWAY PLAY PUBLISHING INC
New York
www.broadwayplaypublishing.com
info@broadwayplaypublishing.com

ALICE IN THE BADLANDS
© Copyright 2018 Julie Marie Myatt

Cover photo by the author

First edition: January 2018
I S B N: 978-0-88145-811-4

Book design: Marie Donovan
Page make-up: Adobe InDesign
Typeface: Palatino

ALICE IN THE BADLANDS was written in Minneapolis in 2002.

CHARACTERS & SETTING

ALICE
The COWBOY
The MAN

The Badlands, South Dakota

ACT ONE

(Sound of a woman breathing O S. She's running.)

(Slide of ALICE *in a car, behind the wheel. Looking behind her. Her hair blowing across her face)*

(Darkness)

(Breathing O S)

(Crying. O S)

(Breathing O S)

(Lights up)

Scene 1

*(*ALICE *enters the stage holding six shooters. She has them out and ready to shoot, looking all around her, scared, ready to kill whatever comes near her.)*

(Scared, she sits down and cries.)

(A rugged COWBOY *enters, holding a gun, pointed at her.)*

ALICE: Go ahead. Kill me. I don't care.
(She continues to cry.)
Shoot me. Right in the head. Go ahead. Make it fast.

(The COWBOY *stares at* ALICE.*)*

ALICE: I don't want to feel a thing. I'm tired of feeling! I'm sure you're a good shot. I'm sure you've killed lots of people. Maybe not women, but I look like shit right now. Don't I?

(The COWBOY *stares.)*

ALICE: It's okay to shoot an ugly woman, isn't it? Let me have it. Right here.
(She points to her head)
Don't make me suffer.

(The COWBOY *shifts his feet.)*

ALICE: Not anymore. I can't take it. I can't. I've had it up to here
(Points to her head)
with everything. I want it all to end. One shot would do it. So. Take aim. And. Let me have it. Right here.

(The COWBOY *scratches his head.)*

ALICE: You wouldn't have to feel guilty about it. Honest. I asked for it, right? I mean, I told you to kill me. There's no harm in that. You'd be doing me a favor. A big fat favor. You'd be saving one woman, who hasn't the energy to even lick her lips in front of an attractive man…and you are an attractive man. Do women tell you that?

(The COWBOY *blushes.)*

ALICE: You've got a nice look. You do. Very sexy. Normally I would probably turn a coy glance your way, or fix my hair or something. But I don't have it in me. I don't. There's reason enough to kill me right there. Apathy.

(The COWBOY *adjusts his hat.)*

ALICE: Normally I'd start to get nervous and fluttery right now but look, I can't even muster up the energy to lick my goddamn lips to tempt you with them…I look like hell. I don't like to kid myself. I want to

die and I want you to kill me. So please. Mister sexy
britches. Blow my brains out. Right here.
(Points to head)
I'm ready for you.

(ALICE waits. The COWBOY doesn't move.)

ALICE: Come on! Do it! I'm miserable! What are you
waiting for?
(She grabs hold of his leg.)
Do it! For Christ's sake!
(She shuts her eyes and points to her head.)
Right here! I'm begging you.

COWBOY: I don't have any bullets.

ALICE: What?

(The COWBOY puts down the gun.)

ALICE: What kind of cowboy are you?

COWBOY: What do you mean?

ALICE: Out here with no bullets?

COWBOY: You've got a gun. Two of them, as a matter
of—

ALICE: So?

COWBOY: Why don't you shoot yourself?

ALICE: Because I'm a COWARD! Isn't that obvious?

COWBOY: No. Not particularly.

ALICE: It is! Look at me! I'm a mess.

COWBOY: I've seen worse—

ALICE: Why the hell are you carrying a gun if you don't
have any bullets?

COWBOY: I'm a pacifist.

ALICE: Is that so?

COWBOY: Yes.

ALICE: Out here in the middle of no where with political ideals in tow.

COWBOY: Yep.

ALICE: You think some bear or cougar is going to give a rat's ass about your ideals?

COWBOY: Probably not.

ALICE: I'll tell you he's not going to. He's gonna kick your tight little ass. And tear up that good-looking face of yours.

COWBOY: If that's what he's got to do, who am I to stop him?

ALICE: Where are you from? California?

COWBOY: No.

ALICE: Where?

COWBOY: Santa Fe.

ALICE: Holy shit, I should have guessed.
(She slowly stands up.)
No fucking bullets...brilliant...of course...Santa Fe... pacifist...fucking cowboy.
(Uses her shirt to wipe her eyes)
(The COWBOY looks ALICE over.)
(She looks him over. She fixes her hair.)

ALICE: So what are you doing out here?

COWBOY: I'm on a silent retreat.

ALICE: Brilliant.

COWBOY: And you?

ALICE: I'm on the run, what does it look like?

COWBOY: Looks like you're having a melt down.

ALICE: I am having a fucking Meltdown! You would too if you'd been on the run for eight days straight. No

one to talk to. No decent food in your belly. No booze.
No decent sex.

(Both ALICE *and the* COWBOY *adjust their clothes.)*

ALICE: I guess you broke your silence.

COWBOY: So to speak.

*(*ALICE *twirls her guns.)*

COWBOY: You should be careful with those.

ALICE: Why?

COWBOY: You might hurt somebody.

ALICE: That's the idea.

COWBOY: What are you on the run from?

ALICE: What am I Not on the run from…Jesus.

COWBOY: The Law?

ALICE: Yes.

COWBOY: What'd you—

ALICE: The law of physics.

COWBOY: Physics.

ALICE: One bad man plus one stupid girl equals one
messed up girl hung by her heals on his god forsaken
rotten heart until she can't stand to look at herself in
the mirror much less the eyes of strangers. Squared.
Equals. Run like hell.

COWBOY: Wow.

ALICE: Yeah.

COWBOY: And here you are.

ALICE: In all my fucking glory. Say, if I gave you my
gun, and I held the handle, would you be willing to—

COWBOY: No.

ALICE: Some cowboy.

(She puts her guns in their holsters.)
So, what kind of ranch you come from? The Holy
Guacamole Chili con Queso Doritos Extra Flavor Pack
Dude ranch?

COWBOY: It's about sixty acres.

ALICE: Of what?

COWBOY: Dirt mostly.

ALICE: No cattle?

COWBOY: I'm a vege—

ALICE: Oh right. Of course. Of course. So what do you
do out there?

COWBOY: I don't know. Live, I guess.

ALICE: What else?

COWBOY: What else is there?

ALICE: You have a "lassie"?

COWBOY: No.

(ALICE looks the COWBOY over.)

ALICE: Do you have a horse?

COWBOY: Yes.

ALICE: Thank god.
(She pulls out a pack of cigarettes.)
For a minute there, I thought I was going to have to
take you back to the toy store where you belong.

*(ALICE begins to light it when the COWBOY takes the match
and lights it for her.)*

ALICE: Well now, aren't you old-fashioned.
(She looks him over, smoking.)
I'd offer you one, but I get the strong impression you
don't smoke.

COWBOY: No.

ALICE: Too bad. Marlboro could make some real money on you.
(She looks him over. Smiles)
So…where you staying?

(The COWBOY *looks around. There's nothing for miles.)*

ALICE: It's a figure of speech. Or pick up line. Depending on your mood—

COWBOY: Under the stars.

ALICE: Of course.

COWBOY: And you?

ALICE: The wilds of South Dakota.

*(*ALICE *and the* COWBOY *look each other over.)*

ALICE: You have a blanket?

COWBOY: I have two.

ALICE: Huh. Well, isn't that disappointing.

COWBOY: Why?

ALICE: You're so prepared.

COWBOY: I always—

ALICE: I'd rather share yours.

COWBOY: Oh.

ALICE: If you're not going to kill me, I mean, it's the least you could do.

COWBOY: What?

ALICE: Fuck me.

(The COWBOY *adjusts his hat. With great discomfort)*

ALICE: You know. Toss a girl a bone. Out here in the cold night. Nothing but odd hills and dirt for miles. And just the two of us. Alone.

COWBOY: What about that man?

(ALICE *obviously flinches at the thought.*)

ALICE: What about him?

COWBOY: Don't you love him?

ALICE: Let's, let's just not talk about that.

COWBOY: Seems to me—

ALICE: Let's not talk about it!

COWBOY: I wouldn't want to confuse things—

ALICE: They couldn't get any more confusing! Could they?
(*She begins to cry again.*)
Jesus.

(*The* COWBOY *looks around.*)

COWBOY: Looks like there's a good camping spot over there. Flat. A little shelter.

(ALICE *nods.*)

COWBOY: I'll make a bed up for you.

ALICE: Just my luck. Get stuck out here with a goddamn gentleman.

(*The* COWBOY *exits.*)

(ALICE *pulls out one of her guns, puts it to her head.*)

Scene 2

(ALICE *and the* COWBOY *lay under the blankets. A distance apart. Lit faintly by the moon*)

(*Slide of* ALICE *naked in a corner of a bedroom, her face tempting the camera. To come closer*)

(ALICE *turns over.*)

COWBOY: You alright over there?

ALICE: Depends on your definition of 'alright'.

COWBOY: You still crying?

ALICE: I think I'm having a momentary dry spell.
Thank you.

COWBOY: I've never heard a woman cry so much.

ALICE: Does it bother you?

COWBOY: No.

ALICE: Good, 'cause there's plenty more where that
came from.

COWBOY: Where's it coming from?

ALICE: Why?

COWBOY: You seem pretty upset.

ALICE: You want to be my therapist?

COWBOY: Not particularly.

ALICE: Then why open a can a big can of worms you
don't care about.

(Silence)

COWBOY: Who said I didn't care about it.

ALICE: Let's just drop it.

(Silence)

COWBOY: What's his name?

(Silence)

ALICE: I'd rather not talk about him.

(Silence)

COWBOY: What's your name?

(ALICE sighs.)

ALICE: You looking for formal introductions?

COWBOY: No.

ALICE: And I thought you weren't interested in playing
therapist—

COWBOY: I'm not—

ALICE: Alice. For Christ's sake.
(She turns over, her face to the sky. Puts her arms under her head)

COWBOY: Nice night, isn't it?

ALICE: Sure.

(Silence)

COWBOY: I thought it was going to rain. But nope. It's clear.

ALICE: Is anything…ever…really…clear?

COWBOY: Well, there's no clouds now, look, and—

ALICE: Never mind.

(Silence)

COWBOY: I've been out here five days and haven't seen a soul. You're the first.

ALICE: Aren't you the lucky one.

COWBOY: Kind of interesting landscape out here, don't you think?

ALICE: I don't see what's so "Bad" about it.

COWBOY: Lots of odd shapes to the hills. I'd always wanted to see it. How about you? Kind of on my list of Natural Wonders. National Parks not to miss. That kind of thing. I've seen just about all of them now. Yellowstone. Yosemite. Zion. Bryce. The Grand Canyon…it really is Grand. Incredible. Have you seen it?

(ALICE sits up.)

COWBOY: Not to be missed really. It's endless. Catch it at sunset if you can. I camped down in the middle. Quite a night. Really, I just never thought that it would be so—

ALICE: Aren't you Not supposed to talk?

(Silence)

COWBOY: I was trying to cheer you up.

ALICE: Oh.

COWBOY: And I admit, after five days, I am kind of—

ALICE: Thanks.

COWBOY: It can make you a little crazy. Not talking to people.

ALICE: Talking isn't always the cure.

(Silence)

COWBOY: I guess not.
(Silence)
What's the cure?

ALICE: Bullet to the head.

COWBOY: Right.

ALICE: If you can get someone to do it.

COWBOY: Or yourself.

ALICE: It's not as easy as it looks.

COWBOY: I guess not.

ALICE: You spend your entire life trying to stay alive, ending it just doesn't come that natural.

COWBOY: I guess not.

ALICE: Not as natural as you'd like to think.

COWBOY: Uh huh.

(Silence)

ALICE: You don't know what the hell I'm talking about.

COWBOY: I've been in love.

ALICE: With who? Preacher's daughter?

COWBOY: No.

ALICE: You probably sent roses, candy, letters, proposals, the whole bit, didn't you?

COWBOY: Maybe.

ALICE: Uh huh.

COWBOY: It still hurt.

ALICE: You don't know what pain is.

COWBOY: How do you know?

ALICE: You've never met Rob.

COWBOY: Rob?

(Silence)

ALICE: Asshole. I hate him.
(She starts to cry again.)

(Slide of ALICE *smiling, happy)*

ALICE: Mother fucker. Cock sucker. Fuck head. Prick.

COWBOY: You loved him that much?

*(*ALICE *cries harder.)*

ALICE: He was perfect.

COWBOY: Sounds it.

ALICE: Most of the time. We were good together. Great together really. Most of the time.

COWBOY: What happened?

ALICE: I don't know.

*(*ALICE *wipes her nose. The* COWBOY *hands her his red bandana from his neck. She looks at it—it's brand new. She smells it.)*

ALICE: Nice cologne.

COWBOY: Thanks—

ALICE: What is that…"Chaps"?

(The COWBOY *nods.)*

ALICE: You bring that along on your 'wilderness odyssey'?

(The COWBOY *blushes.)*

COWBOY: They make a travel size.

ALICE: Convenient.

(The COWBOY *nods.)*

ALICE: I mean, you don't want to get caught out here in the dark without an attractive smell. Something to woo the ladies. A fragrant lure—

COWBOY: I like it—it makes me feel good.

ALICE: Of course it does.
(She smells the bandana again and blows her nose.)
Makes me feel pretty good too.
(She winks at him.)

COWBOY: Is that all you think about?

ALICE: Sometimes.
(She smells the bandana.)
Rob had a nice smell. Warm. Homey.
(She blows her nose again.)

ALICE: Fucker.

COWBOY: So what happened?

ALICE: To what?

COWBOY: You two.

*(*ALICE *shrugs. Holds the bandana to her nose.)*

ALICE: Are you sure you don't want to fuck me?

(The COWBOY *looks* ALICE *over.)*

ALICE: Is there something about me you find unattractive?

COWBOY: No.

ALICE: Then what's the problem?

COWBOY: You're in love with someone else.

ALICE: So?

COWBOY: It wouldn't be any fun.

ALICE: Says who?
(Silence)
I think it would be lots of fun. Out here in the starry sky. Not a soul for miles. Moon light. A delicate hint of "Chaps" in the air.

(The COWBOY *turns over, covers himself with the blanket.)*

COWBOY: Go to sleep.

ALICE: I can't.

COWBOY: Why not?

(Slide of ALICE *sleeping in Rob's arms. [His face is hidden from the camera.])*

ALICE: I'm lonely.

Scene 3

(A MAN *in a suit and tie enters, searches the stage, and keeps walking.)*

Scene 4

(The COWBOY *sleeps.)*

(Slide of ALICE *reaching)*

*(*ALICE *paces back and forth, smoking, watching the* COWBOY.*)*

(She picks up his hat from the ground and puts it on.)

(She kneels down beside him and touches his face. She moves her hand inside the blanket, then slowly farther down.)

(The COWBOY *grabs her hand, stopping her. He looks at her, then lets go of her hand. Grabs the hat from her head.)*

*(*ALICE *backs away.)*

Scene 5

(Morning)

(The COWBOY *sits with a small stove, a coffee pot on top.)*

*(*ALICE *wakes and quickly exits.)*

(Slide of ALICE *unzipping her pants.)*

*(*ALICE *enters the stage zipping her pants.)*

ALICE: Morning.

COWBOY: Morning.

ALICE: Sleep okay?

COWBOY: I slept fine.

ALICE: Good. Glad to hear it. So, where you off to today?

COWBOY: I haven't decided.

ALICE: More silence?

COWBOY: I suppose.

*(*ALICE *helps herself to a cup of coffee.)*

ALICE: That's something to look forward to.

COWBOY: What?

*(*ALICE *looks around them.)*

ALICE: A day of nothing but rocks. Miles and miles of rocks.

COWBOY: Where are you going?

ALICE: I'm searching my grave sight.

COWBOY: Right.

ALICE: I think someplace over there may work. Looks ominous enough.

COWBOY: Wait till the sun hits it.

ALICE: Why?

COWBOY: It won't look ominous any longer. It will be stunning. A sight too beautiful to kill yourself.

ALICE: I'll wait for the sun to go down.

COWBOY: But after all that beauty, sweeping over you like that, would you really want to—

ALICE: Hey, why don't you just start that silence part right now. Huh? Give another stab at it. I won't stop you.

COWBOY: Would you?

ALICE: What do you care, Lone Ranger?

COWBOY: Just seems a pity—

ALICE: You don't find me so goddamn beautiful, so I guess it's no great loss—

COWBOY: I didn't say I don't find you beautiful.

ALICE: Well, let's just say, you had your chance.

COWBOY: Romantic.

ALICE: Could have been.

COWBOY: Not like that.

ALICE: I bet you just like to call all the shots.

COWBOY: Maybe.

ALICE: A girl can't wait all day.
(*She drinks her coffee down. Gathers her things*)
Well, been nice sleeping with you. Could have been magic, but you know.

COWBOY: You're leaving?

ALICE: Look, I am out here to off myself—

COWBOY: So you say—

ALICE: Don't you think a little carnal pleasure before I enter the next world was extremely little to ask?

COWBOY: I don't know—

ALICE: What's a girl got to do to get laid these days? Christ. Seems pretty simple to me. Men used to jump at the chance. But now, now you gotta be in love. Gotta be head over heals. Gotta have a plan. What ever happened to a good old-fashioned sweaty fuck in the wilderness? Huh?

COWBOY: Well, people get attached—

ALICE: So what?!

COWBOY: Well—

ALICE: What's wrong with that?

COWBOY: Someone gets hurt—

ALICE: I'm already hurt!

COWBOY: Still—

(ALICE *sits on the* COWBOY'*s lap.*)

ALICE: You wouldn't have to worry about that. My heart's already been broken. Believe me. It's shattered, mister. I got shards cutting across every inch of my body right now. All I'm asking you to do is ease the pain—

COWBOY: I'm not that kind of—

ALICE: Don't you see? You'd be just a moment's salve on my wounds—

COWBOY: I'm not that kind of man.

(*The* COWBOY *lifts* ALICE *off him.*)

COWBOY: Anymore.

ALICE: Who are you—

COWBOY: I've changed my ways—

ALICE: Gary Cooper?

COWBOY: Ever see "High Noon"?

ALICE: Sure.

COWBOY: Cooper was great in that—

ALICE: I cheered for the bad guys.

(*The* COWBOY *begins to fold the blankets.*)

COWBOY: Which way you walking?

(ALICE *touches her guns.*)

COWBOY: There's a path that way.

ALICE: So there is.

COWBOY: It's safer to stay on the path.

(ALICE *twirls one of her guns.*)

ALICE: I'm not looking for safety.
(*She sticks the gun in her mouth. Suggestively*)

COWBOY: Stay on the path.

(ALICE *pulls the gun out of her mouth.*)

ALICE: What are you going to do if I don't?

(ALICE *smiles. She exits in the opposite direction of the path.*)

(*The* COWBOY *watches her go.*)

Scene 6

(*Slide of* ALICE *pulling off her shirt*)

(ALICE *enters walking backwards, twirling her guns. She stops. Waits. She turns and exits.*)

(*The* COWBOY *enters. Follows* ALICE. *Exits*)

Scene 7

(The MAN *in the suit enters, searches, exits.)*

Scene 8

(Slide of ALICE *grabbing a man's hand)*
(The COWBOY *enters, looking for* ALICE. *He exits.)*

Scene 9

(Slide of ALICE *opening a door)*
(The COWBOY *stands drinking from a canteen.)*
*(*ALICE *enters. It's hot. She wipes her neck. Her dry mouth)*
ALICE: That doesn't say, "Drink Me", does it?
(The COWBOY *looks at the canteen.)*
COWBOY: No.
ALICE: Oh.
(The COWBOY *offers* ALICE *the canteen.)*
ALICE: Liquor?
COWBOY: No.
ALICE: Poison?
COWBOY: No.
ALICE: Thank you, no.
COWBOY: Take it.
ALICE: No.
COWBOY: You shouldn't mess around with this heat.
ALICE: Will it kill me?
COWBOY: Yes. But it won't be pretty.
ALICE: Huh.

COWBOY: You just walked eight miles out of your way.

ALICE: Did I?

COWBOY: Yes.

ALICE: And what was my way?

COWBOY: You're not out here to kill yourself.

ALICE: I'm not?

COWBOY: You just want the attention.

ALICE: From who?

COWBOY: I don't know. Whoever. This Rob guy.

ALICE: If I just wanted attention, you think I'd come all the way fuck out here to off myself? Don't you think I'd find a place a little closer to home?

COWBOY: No.

ALICE: Why not?

COWBOY: Less dramatic. More pathetic. This offers some romance to it all.

ALICE: Really?

COWBOY: I think so.

ALICE: So you think killing myself at the feet of the man who just told me he wasn't in love with me would be pathetic?

COWBOY: Yes. Tragic, but pathetic—

ALICE: I couldn't agree more.

COWBOY: I know I wouldn't like it—

ALICE: This way, he doesn't know anything about it. He doesn't even know that I'm upset. He doesn't have to see my crying and carrying on like a sack of shit. He doesn't have to know a word.

COWBOY: Until they find you dead.

ALICE: Exactly.

COWBOY: A desperate cry for help.

ALICE: No—

COWBOY: Why do you need so much attention?

ALICE: Listen, Bronco Billy, you said you didn't want to be my therapist, so don't follow me around just to throw these little two bit psychological questions at me when you have no real interest in the answer.

(The COWBOY *drinks more water.)*

COWBOY: I was a psych major.

ALICE: I studied nuclear physics and look how far it got me.

COWBOY: I could be of some help.

ALICE: I already asked you for "some help" and you turned me down.

COWBOY: Real help.

ALICE: Look, that's real to me. I haven't been—I haven't had—

COWBOY: What?

*(*ALICE *starts to cry again.)*

ALICE: Nothing.

COWBOY: He wouldn't sleep with you?

*(*ALICE *shakes her head "no".)*

COWBOY: Why not?

ALICE: He's in love with someone else—

(Slide of ALICE *kicking a door down.)*

ALICE: I thought that if he just spent enough time with me, see how great I was, that he'd get over her…and he got close, he really did…but he never did. Not really. Fucker.

COWBOY: That is tragic.

ALICE: And the more he kept me away, the more I wanted him. The more determined I was to win him over. Asshole.

COWBOY: That happens a lot—

ALICE: I would push myself on him, over and over again. Until finally I got him in bed, and, and—

COWBOY: What?

ALICE: Nothing happened. He wouldn't touch me.

COWBOY: Why not—

ALICE: Because he wasn't in love with me! Jesus. How many times do I have to say it! You trying to rub salt in the wound!

COWBOY: No.

ALICE: And then I repel you!

COWBOY: You didn't—

ALICE: What kind of woman am I?

COWBOY: Confused.

(ALICE *blows her nose in her sleeve.*)

ALICE: Was it freshman psych you learned that?

COWBOY: What happened with your father?

ALICE: What?

COWBOY: You have father issues, don't you.

(ALICE *studies the* COWBOY.)

COWBOY: Did he make you feel insignificant?

(ALICE *sits back.*)

COWBOY: Invisible?

(ALICE *smiles.*)

COWBOY: Unlovable—

ALICE: Say—

COWBOY: What?

ALICE: Which one of us, between you and me, is dressed up like Roy Rogers?

COWBOY: I don't want to kill myself.

ALICE: Yet.

COWBOY: I don't fall in love with the wrong men.

ALICE: You are just a few fellows short of the Village People.

COWBOY: Let's talk about your father.

(ALICE *lights a cigarette.*)

ALICE: Why don't you silently retreat.

COWBOY: My friends say I'm quite good.

ALICE: What friends? Pa and Little Jo?

COWBOY: People come to me for—

ALICE: Well, I'm not coming to you, am I? I've got a plan out here and I'm going to stick to it. You can follow me all the way to North Dakota, I don't care, but eventually, I'm gonna find the courage to end all this and you aren't going to stop me... A woman can only take so much.
(*She starts to cry again.*)

ALICE: I can only take so much rejection in one lifetime.

COWBOY: That's got Daddy written all over it.

(ALICE *pulls out one of her guns.*)

ALICE: You're going to be crying for Daddy in a minute if you don't shut your trap.

COWBOY: Why kill me?

(ALICE *cocks the pistol.*)

ALICE: Practice.

(The COWBOY *takes off his hat. Waits. He licks his lips.*
Pushes back his hair. Looking more sexy)

ALICE: Don't try and distract me.

COWBOY: Am I?
(He squints his eyes.)

ALICE: I mean it.

COWBOY: What?

ALICE: You're teasing me.

COWBOY: What?

ALICE: You're just standing there teasing me.

COWBOY: Says who?

*(*ALICE *smiles and turns the gun, puts it her mouth.)*

(She pulls the trigger. At the same time, the COWBOY *covers*
his eyes.)

(Click. Nothing happens. The gun is empty.)

*(*ALICE *watches as the* COWBOY *uncovers his eyes. She takes*
the gun from her mouth. Wipes her mouth and laughs.)

ALICE: Cowards.

Scene 10

*(*MAN *in the suit stops, lights a cigarette, checks his map,*
and keeps walking.)

Scene 11

(Slide of ALICE *staring straight ahead.)*

(The COWBOY *has ripped both* ALICE's *guns from her and*
puts them in his back pack.)

ALICE: That's really not necessary.

COWBOY: I think it is.

ALICE: Well, you lean on the conservative side. Don't you.

COWBOY: You're an idiot.

ALICE: I agree. I should have brought more bullets.

COWBOY: Stupid—

ALICE: Was a waste shooting at rabbits. They have a lot of holes to hide in out here.

COWBOY: Start walking.

ALICE: What?

COWBOY: Start walking.

ALICE: No.

COWBOY: I'm getting you out of here.

ALICE: Really.

COWBOY: Alive.

ALICE: Really?

COWBOY: Start walking.

(ALICE *sits down.*)

(*The* COWBOY *points his gun at her.*)

COWBOY: Start walking.

(ALICE *laughs.*)

ALICE: What you gonna shoot me with? Kisses?

(*The* COWBOY *takes bullets out of his pocket and puts them in his gun.*)

COWBOY: Start walking.

ALICE: Well. Now.

(*The* COWBOY *cocks the gun.*)

COWBOY: Start. Walking.

ALICE: My hero.
(*She lies down on the ground.*)
Come get me.

(*The* COWBOY *reaches down and grabs her, pulling her up with one pull.*)

COWBOY: I said—

(ALICE *laughs.*)

ALICE: Wow—

COWBOY: Start—

ALICE: I like you.

COWBOY: Walking.

(ALICE *takes one step. Stops*)

ALICE: What's your name?

COWBOY: What?

ALICE: I don't know your name.

COWBOY: Walt.

ALICE: Walt?

COWBOY: Yes.

ALICE: That's nice.

COWBOY: Thank you.

(ALICE *takes a few more steps. Stops*)

ALICE: Are you gonna save me, Walt?

COWBOY: Yes.

ALICE: Then what?

COWBOY: What?

ALICE: What are you gonna do with me?

COWBOY: What?

ALICE: Who are you saving me for?

COWBOY: Yourself.

ALICE: Oh.
(She takes one step. Stops)
But, Walt.

(The COWBOY *sighs loudly.)*

ALICE: Am I testing your patience, Walt?

(The COWBOY *adjusts his hat.* ALICE *laughs.)*

ALICE: Imagine living with me. Would I not be exhausting? …See, here's the thing… If you're saving me *for* myself…you're wasting your time. Are you saving me *for* or *from* myself?

COWBOY: Both.

ALICE: Yeah. That's what I thought. Damn.

COWBOY: Just get moving—

ALICE: Big mistake, Walt. Big mistake. Either way, I am stuck with myself and that's a problem. That's a real problem.
(She holds out her arms. Ready)
Go ahead and shoot.

COWBOY: No.

ALICE: I don't want me.

COWBOY: I think you do.

ALICE: I don't. I'm done with me. Had enough. I'm throwing in the towel—

COWBOY: No—

ALICE: "Alice doesn't want to live here anymore."

COWBOY: Let me show you something.

ALICE: Will it change my life?

COWBOY: Maybe—
(He reaches for something in his back pack.)

ALICE: I read the *Celestine Prophecy* twice and got absolutely nothing. Zip.

COWBOY: Where is it...

(*He sets his gun down and gets on his knees, searching through his pack.*)

(ALICE *tries to grab the gun, but the* COWBOY *gets to it before she can.*)

ALICE: You're pretty quick for a Rhinestone Cowboy.

(*The* COWBOY *finally finds what he was looking for. He holds it out for* ALICE *on bended knee.*)

ALICE: Oh my, what is it? An engagement ring? I do! I do—

(*The*COWBOY *opens his hand. It's a small jaw bone.*)

(ALICE *pulls back.*)

ALICE: What the fuck is that?

COWBOY: My daughter.

ALICE: What?

COWBOY: What's left of her.

ALICE: What...

COWBOY: Killed by a stranger. And left in the woods.

ALICE: Get that away from me.

COWBOY: This was all they found.

ALICE: Shit.

COWBOY: To identify her.

ALICE: Could you put it away?

COWBOY: This is all I have.

ALICE: Please.

(*The* COWBOY *examines the bone.*)

COWBOY: She didn't have a chance.

ALICE: Jesus.

COWBOY: Four years old.
(*He puts the bone in his back pack.*)

ALICE: That's terrible.

COWBOY: I know.

ALICE: Carrying that around with you.

COWBOY: What do you want me to do with it?

ALICE: Bury it.

COWBOY: Why?

ALICE: It's disturbing.

COWBOY: Maybe.

ALICE: Shit.

COWBOY: You think death is romantic.

ALICE: I don't—

COWBOY: I think you are a spoiled brat.
(ALICE *lights a cigarette.*)

ALICE: Really?

COWBOY: You would break someone's heart.

ALICE: You think so?

COWBOY: I guarantee it.

ALICE: Is that so terrible?

COWBOY: Yes.

ALICE: Huh…I kind of like that idea.

COWBOY: Selfish bitch.

ALICE: Yeah.

COWBOY: You're someone's daughter.

ALICE: Yeah?

COWBOY: You'll hurt him.

ALICE: I'm not four years old.

COWBOY: So?

ALICE: My bones are big.

COWBOY: Listen—

ALICE: And beginning to rot.

(The COWBOY *points his gun at* ALICE.*)*

COWBOY: Get moving.

ALICE: No.

(The COWBOY *scratches his head.)*

ALICE: *(Laughing)* Kind of quandary, isn't it—

(The COWBOY *knocks* ALICE *in the head with his gun. She goes unconscious.)*

Scene 12

(The MAN *in the suit finds* ALICE's *cigarette butt on the ground, and follows the trail.)*

Scene 13

(Slide of ALICE *thrashing her apartment.)*

(The COWBOY *carries* ALICE *on his shoulder, and sets her down on the ground. The sun is beginning to set.)*

*(*ALICE's *shoulder shows, as her shirt falls off her. Part of her breast can be seen.)*

(The COWBOY *takes off his back pack. He takes off his shirt. His boots. Then he takes off his pants. Looking at* ALICE *all the while)*

(He moves toward her, removing his underwear.)

Scene 14

(The MAN *in the suit checks his compass in the back of the stage.)*

(He searches. Finally yells)

MAN: Alice!

Scene 15

(Slide of ALICE *holding onto a man's back)*

*(*ALICE *wakes, alone on stage. She feels her head, looks around. Sits up)*

(The COWBOY *enters with a dead rabbit in his hand.)*

COWBOY: Hungry?

ALICE: What?

COWBOY: I found this.

ALICE: I don't want it.

COWBOY: It's nice and fat.

*(*ALICE *touches her head. Looking for blood)*

ALICE: Did you have to hit me?

COWBOY: What?

ALICE: Did you have to hit me?

COWBOY: I didn't hit you.

ALICE: You did.

COWBOY: You fell asleep.

ALICE: Then what's this knot on my head?

COWBOY: Ignorance.

ALICE: You're a funny one.

(She begins to shift. Begins to stand. Can't get up. Yet)

I think we're beginning to understand each other.

COWBOY: You think so?

ALICE: Yeah.

COWBOY: How's that?

(ALICE *tries to light a cigarette.*)

ALICE: What are you running from?

(*The* COWBOY *inspects the rabbit.*)

ALICE: Indians?

(ALICE *laughs. The* COWBOY *still doesn't respond.*)

ALICE: I thought you were a vegetarian.

COWBOY: I cheat. Sometimes.

ALICE: Uh huh. Listen. Walt.
(*She begins to stand up. She notices something is different about her clothes.*)
Walt...

COWBOY: I'm going to skin this.

ALICE: What?

COWBOY: I'm going to skin this. Over there. The coyotes will smell it. Then I'll cook it up for you.

ALICE: I don't want it.

COWBOY: You need to eat.

ALICE: How long was I out?

COWBOY: What?

ALICE: How long was I out?

COWBOY: I don't know.

ALICE: What?

COWBOY: I didn't time it.

ALICE: What did you do?

COWBOY: What?

ALICE: While I was out?

COWBOY: I'm gonna go skin this.

ALICE: Walt?

COWBOY: I'm gonna do it over there.

ALICE: Do it here.

COWBOY: You don't want to see it.

ALICE: I do.

COWBOY: It's not pretty.

ALICE: I want to see it.

COWBOY: You don't.

ALICE: I do.

COWBOY: Why?

ALICE: I don't like being kept in the dark.

COWBOY: It's bloody.

ALICE: So?

COWBOY: You'll see me rip into it.

ALICE: So?

COWBOY: It's brutal. Really.

ALICE: Good.

COWBOY: Messy.

ALICE: What did you do while I was out, Walt?

COWBOY: Watched you.

ALICE: Watched me what?

COWBOY: Sleep.

ALICE: Really?

COWBOY: Yes.

ALICE: How'd I look?

COWBOY: Peaceful.

ALICE: Really?

COWBOY: Sure.

ALICE: I doubt that.

COWBOY: Why?

ALICE: I toss.

COWBOY: Huh.

ALICE: I turn.

COWBOY: I didn't notice.

ALICE: I mumble things I shouldn't.

COWBOY: Huh.

ALICE: I dream.

COWBOY: You were unconscious.

ALICE: Was I?

COWBOY: Yes.

ALICE: Huh.

COWBOY: It was for your own good.

ALICE: Really.

COWBOY: I'm going to go skin this.

ALICE: Why am I wet?

COWBOY: What?

ALICE: Must have been a good dream.

COWBOY: I don't know.

ALICE: Did you notice?

COWBOY: What?

ALICE: If I enjoyed it?

COWBOY: What?

ALICE: The dream.

COWBOY: No.

ALICE: Walt?

COWBOY: What?

ALICE: What did you do while I was dreaming?

COWBOY: I watched you.
(He exits.)

(ALICE stands up. To watch. She knows there is something different about her.)

(She watches the COWBOY skin the rabbit. And buttons her blouse.)

Scene 16

(The MAN in the suit sees something in the distance, he smells the air. He walks toward it.)

Scene 17

(Slide of ALICE swallowing pills)

(ALICE and the COWBOY sit eating the rabbit, the fire in front of them.)

(The sun is setting.)

ALICE: This really isn't bad.

COWBOY: I told you.

(ALICE chews the meat from the bone.)

ALICE: I feel wild.

(The COWBOY eats.)

ALICE: Do you?

COWBOY: What?

ALICE: Stark.

(The COWBOY *shrugs.)*

ALICE: Let's take our clothes off and eat.

COWBOY: Why?

ALICE: A kind of bacchanal.

COWBOY: It's cold.

*(*ALICE *puts down the meat and takes off her clothes—down to her underwear.)*

ALICE: Some cowboy.
(She resumes eating the rabbit.)
You wouldn't last one day out on the Real range, you know it?

COWBOY: I'm the one feeding you.

ALICE: I didn't ask you to.

COWBOY: You'll thank me. Some day.

ALICE: Don't hold your breath.
(Silence)
Tell me something.

COWBOY: If I have to.

ALICE: That bone…was there a mother for that daughter?

(The COWBOY *looks* ALICE *over.)*

ALICE: Am I getting too personal?

COWBOY: Yes.

ALICE: What happened to her?

(The COWBOY *is quiet.)*

ALICE: Your retreat is over, pal.
(She keeps her eye on him.)

COWBOY: It didn't work out.

ALICE: Why not?

COWBOY: It just didn't.

ALICE: You cheat on her?

COWBOY: No.

ALICE: She leave you for someone else?

COWBOY: You might say that.

ALICE: I might?

COWBOY: Yes.

ALICE: How might I say it?

COWBOY: It didn't work out.

ALICE: And your daughter?

COWBOY: What about her?

ALICE: She get over that?

COWBOY: I guess so.

ALICE: You guess so?

COWBOY: It didn't work out.

ALICE: You've got a little edge to you, don't you?

COWBOY: You're rubbing off on me.

ALICE: I do have that affect on people. Kind of like cheap perfume. You're not sure if it's familiar because you like it or you can't stand the smell of it.

COWBOY: Maybe.

ALICE: Rob tried to get rid of me several times. But I wouldn't have it. I rubbed myself all over his skin. Over and over again. I covered him with…
(She puts down the meat.)

ALICE: Let me ask you something.

COWBOY: You already did.

ALICE: You think I'm crazy?

COWBOY: I think you're stupid.

ALICE: I didn't ask you that. Besides, I'm as smart as they come. Believe me.
(She taps her head.)
This thing's a whip. It could take you down in a second...leave you shaking...make you laugh so hard you pee your pants...but that doesn't mean shit sometimes, does it?

COWBOY: Maybe not—

ALICE: And being smart enough to see how stupid you're being can—well...there comes a time to blow those fucking whirling brains out. I mean it. The precocious girl's come undone. I'm tossing in the towel on this turd of heart. Yep. Philadelphia's favorite liberty Bell has cracked open for the last time...there's nothing left for me there but my father's disappointment—and don't start with your Bachelors third degree. I don't want to hear it...I was destined for great things, you know? I was graduated, promoted and adorned with honors. My whole life. I'm was a hot shot executive. Do you believe that?

COWBOY: No.

ALICE: I know! But really. It's true. Two weeks ago you wouldn't have recognized me, Walt. Really...You like a woman in a suit? You find that sexy?

COWBOY: I don't—

ALICE: I walked out on Big Business. I did. The Drug business. Huge company. Anti-depressants. Big money. Big business. Ever take 'em?

COWBOY: No—

ALICE: They work wonders. Look at me—
(She laughs.)
I told people what to do. I made deals. Some young nervous Dartmouth graduate made my phone calls for me. She would get me coffee. And I enjoyed making

her sweat…push a smile…rattle around me…watching
her want my approval…I loved it… And I have a great
apartment too. High ceilings. View of downtown.

COWBOY: Nice.

ALICE: Luxury living.

COWBOY: Great.

ALICE: Someone else will enjoy it now. Maybe my sister
will take it. She's hardworking. Stable. A lesbian.

COWBOY: Really.

ALICE: I want to come back and be a man. You know it?
Give me a pecker.

COWBOY: What would that do for you?

ALICE: I don't know.

COWBOY: You don't know—

ALICE: Do I seem rational to you?

COWBOY: No—

ALICE: Just seems being a smart girl with a dumb heart
is worse than being a dumb man with a hungry pecker.
The hungry pecker is pure. Raw energy. Simple thing.
Animal thrust. But this dumb heart is too clumsy and
eager. Remedial. Muddy and desperate. It's like it
has eight desperate arms but just one finger. A pinky
finger. My brain can't do anything with it but tote it
around like fucking useless pointer or a flailing sack of
shit. But if I cut it out, my brain will miss it. It's become
my stupid blind, smelly companion… And I hate it.

COWBOY: Sorry to hear that.

ALICE: I'm stuck.

COWBOY: It's a phase.

(ALICE *looks at the* COWBOY.)

ALICE: Can I tell you something?

COWBOY: Do I have a choice?

ALICE: You haven't told me one goddamn bit of interesting advice. No real words of wisdom. No epiphanies to bank on. No sage-like truths. Nothing. Outside those bullets, that bonk on the head and that jaw bone, you're really not very compelling.

(*The* COWBOY *stares at* ALICE.)

ALICE: Really. How long have we known each other... twenty-four...thirty-six hours...and you haven't said or done one goddamn thing that has surprised me. Not one. That's depressing.

COWBOY: You're a fucking cunt, you know it?

ALICE: I've been told. That it's part of my charm.

COWBOY: Rob was a smart man.

ALICE: You think so?

COWBOY: I wouldn't touch you either.

ALICE: Really?

COWBOY: Not with a ten foot pole.
(*He resumes eating.*)

ALICE: You're right...it wasn't ten feet...but you were hard enough, weren't you?

COWBOY: What?

ALICE: You should open your eyes.

COWBOY: Why?

ALICE: You would have seen me smiling.

COWBOY: I don't know what you're talking about.

ALICE: Don't worry, Walt. I'll be taking it to my grave.

COWBOY: What?

ALICE: The Chaps on my hide.
(*She smells her shoulder.*)

I really do feel like I've been out on the plains. Rode hard. Just like those commercials. Dusty breezes. Stained denim. Very Western. I can almost smell the horse shit.

(She laughs.)

Giddy up.

COWBOY: I don't know—

(ALICE laughs again.)

ALICE: You've spent way too much time on your higher self, Walt. Come back to the depths.

(She winks at him.)

I'm much too clever for you. This could get boring—

(The COWBOY slaps ALICE across the face.)

COWBOY: Another word, and I'm going to shove this gun up your ass and blow that goddamn smart mouth straight through the canyon.

ALICE: What's stopping you?

COWBOY: Not much—

ALICE: Good. Now we're getting somewhere.

COWBOY: Shut up.

(ALICE smiles.)

ALICE: Walt?

COWBOY: I said, shut up.

ALICE: But Walt….Walt…*Walt*?

COWBOY: What?

ALICE: I like it when you're angry.

COWBOY: Fuck you.

ALICE: You're really quite beautiful…when you're upset.

(The COWBOY points the gun at ALICE's face.)

COWBOY: Shut. Up.

ALICE: Stunning.

(The COWBOY *cocks the gun.)*

*(*ALICE *slips off her underwear.)*

ALICE: Really. I'm sorry. But. You're suddenly. Just. So. Gorgeous. I'm overwhelmed.

*(*ALICE *moves toward the* COWBOY *as the* MAN *in the suit enters; exhausted, wrinkled and dirty.)*

MAN: Alice.

*(*ALICE *turns and sees the* MAN. *She quickly covers her body.)*

ALICE: Daddy.

END OF ACT ONE

ACT TWO

Scene 1

(Slide of ALICE *as a little girl. Showing her panties to the camera.)*

*(*ALICE *is dressed, sitting slumped and embarrassed. The* MAN *in the suit, [her father], sits smoking, and the* COWBOY *stares at the sky, his gun on the ground.)*

MAN: I just don't get it.

COWBOY: Nice night coming in.

MAN: I don't.

COWBOY: Stars everywhere, huh? You can't beat that.

MAN: A grown woman, my daughter, so goddamn fucked up. It's embarrassing.

COWBOY: The little dipper.

MAN: Where did I go wrong?

COWBOY: The big dipper.

MAN: Huh?

COWBOY: I don't remember what that's called over there.

MAN: Tell me what I did wrong.

COWBOY: Gosh, it's right on the tip of my tongue.

MAN: What did I do wrong with you?

COWBOY: Right on the tip of my tongue.

MAN: I gave you everything, didn't I?

COWBOY: I should remember this stuff.

MAN: You had the best of everything.

COWBOY: Astronomy's important out in the wild.

MAN: The best schools.

COWBOY: Gotta be able to follow the stars.

MAN: The best clothes.

COWBOY: They'll show you the way through anything.

MAN: The best vacations.

COWBOY: Hell or high water.

MAN: Ponies.

COWBOY: They'll show you the way through the night.

MAN: Doll houses.

COWBOY: Anywhere.

MAN: Birds. I hate birds. But I gave them to you, didn't I?

(ALICE *lights a cigarette.*)

COWBOY: That's a map up there, you know.

MAN: Fucking love birds. Were on each other all the time. Getting off. Squawking.

COWBOY: Endless.

MAN: I even cleaned up the bird shit when I had to, just so you could keep the stupid things. Did you know that?

COWBOY: A big bold map of the world.

MAN: Gave up my *Wall Street Journal* some mornings just to line that damn birds' cage so you wouldn't get in trouble with your mother. Did you know that?

COWBOY: It's glorious, isn't it?

MAN: One bird bit my finger. I still have a scar.

COWBOY: This is what it's all about out here.

MAN: But I didn't say a word, did I, because you wanted the damn things. You begged me for the fucking things. You couldn't keep your eyes off them. And I wanted you to be happy.

COWBOY: Vast beauty.

MAN: All I wanted was for you to be happy.

ALICE: Bull shit.

MAN: What?

ALICE: Nothing.

COWBOY: Ahh…

MAN: Did you hear that?

COWBOY: What?

MAN: My daughter. She's got a mouth on her.

COWBOY: I know.

MAN: She's a fucking mess.

COWBOY: I know.

MAN: What do you think I should do?

COWBOY: Hug her.

MAN: What?

COWBOY: Tell her you love her.

MAN: What?

COWBOY: Make her feel important.

(Silence)

MAN: Who the hell are you?

ALICE: He's an idiot.

MAN: That's obvious.

ALICE: Isn't it?

MAN: Come morning, I'm getting you out of here, Alice, and we're going to get you straightened out. Once and for all.

ALICE: Really?

MAN: Damn straight.

ALICE: How's that?

MAN: You don't worry about the details. I got it all worked out.

ALICE: What?

MAN: It's all taken care of.

ALICE: What?

MAN: I got the best shrinks in the country this time, ready to talk to you.

ALICE: Is that right?

MAN: They're gonna straighten you out. Do what they have to do.

ALICE: Oh?

MAN: Sure. They're gonna use all their expertise. All their doo dads and gadgets and electrodes and brain washing and body scrubbing...hell, maybe even twist you like a pretzel if they have to.

ALICE: Fun.

MAN: But get to the bottom of this charade.

ALICE: Really?

MAN: Straighten you out again.

ALICE: Really?

MAN: Best men in the country.

ALICE: Great.

MAN: At your disposal.

ALICE: Really.

MAN: I am not going to let my daughter spend her life running away from trouble. Acting dramatic. Sulking in her shorts. I am not.

ALICE: That's why I love you, Dad—

MAN: You can waste your mother's time, Lord knows, that woman thrives on pissing away endless hours curled up on that sofa watching so called "educational" television—she was the smartest woman in her entire class, you know—

ALICE: I know—

MAN: I don't know what happened—

ALICE: She married you—

MAN: And all those boys you chase…Jesus Christ…I don't know where you find those nare-do-wells. Under the bridge? You wake them up from the gutters and give them your number?

ALICE: Good one, Dad—

MAN: Might as well just hang out at the homeless shelter and hand out flyers. Welcome to your next relationship—

ALICE: Good idea.

MAN: And this guy. Who's he—

ALICE: My American Dream.

MAN: A decent man and dedicated father just shouldn't have to see his daughter naked like that— hell—

ALICE: I suppose.

MAN: But I am telling you, Alice, you are not going to waste your life under my clock. No you are not.

ALICE: Sure thing, Dad.

MAN: I've spent too much money building you up and—shit—your I Q is way above genius, did I ever tell you that?

ALICE: Yes.

MAN: You're a smart cookie.

ALICE: Crumbled—

MAN: I just don't get it. But hell, I don't claim to understand you, do I?

ALICE: No.

MAN: I don't. But I love you. I guess I don't have to understand you. Not one bit. But I do love you, Alice.

ALICE: So I'm told.

MAN: And I'm gonna get you back on track.

COWBOY: May I make a suggestion?

MAN: What's with the outfit?

ALICE: Got me.

MAN: I keep waiting for Tonto to ride in.

(ALICE *laughs.*)

(*The* COWBOY *is quiet.*)

ALICE: Tonto! God! Yes! I've been racking my brain to remember his name. Thanks, Dad.

MAN: You shooting a film out here?

COWBOY: No.

MAN: Trying out a Halloween get up?

COWBOY: No.

MAN: What gives?

COWBOY: It's comfortable.

MAN: Ever try sweat pants?

(ALICE *laughs, loving this.*)

COWBOY: This is durable.

MAN: So's rubber, but you don't see me walking around in radial tires, do you?

ALICE: Great.

MAN: It's just seems impractical.

COWBOY: So does a suit.

ALICE: He's got you there, Dad.

COWBOY: And those shoes. Loafers?

MAN: I, I wasn't expecting to come out here.

COWBOY: I guess not.

MAN: I didn't plan for camping.

COWBOY: Obviously.

MAN: But hell. I don't understand her, but I know my daughter's ways. I can find her trail. Can't I?

COWBOY: So it appears.

MAN: I've tracked her down across this goddamn country fifteen times.

COWBOY: Fifteen times?

MAN: Been pulling this shit since she was thirteen.

COWBOY: Really?

MAN: Ran off with some kids in a polka dot school bus. I had to peel her off some stoned hippy's lap and take her home.

ALICE: The good old days.

MAN: I've seen things no father should have to see.

ALICE: His name was Sky.

MAN: One time I found her living in a tree in the Red Wood Forest. She was eating bald eagles and sleeping with a communist.

ALICE: Red. He was a good man—

MAN: Even found her in the Ozarks. That was something.

ALICE: Wow.

MAN: Ever seen a man with a tail?

COWBOY: No.

MAN: You'll never forget it.

ALICE: No you won't.

MAN: Disgusting.

ALICE: Delicious.

MAN: I've got trouble on my hands. Always have. Her sister's an angel. She's a lesbian.

ALICE: I already told him.

MAN: I'm not crazy about the hair cut, but a lot less hassle than this one.

COWBOY: I had a daughter.

MAN: Did you? What happen? The Engines get her—

ALICE: Dad—

MAN: What?

ALICE: She's dead.

MAN: Oh.
(He pulls a small flask from his pocket. Takes a drink)

ALICE: Yeah.

MAN: I'm sorry.
(To the COWBOY*)*
I am sorry.

(The COWBOY *pulls out the bone.)*

ALICE: Please don't show that thing again—

MAN: Hell.

Cowboy: I know.

Man: What happened?

Cowboy: She was crazy about men.

Man: Damn.

Cowboy: She'd follow them anywhere.

(The Man *in the suit holds out his hand to the* Cowboy.*)*

Man: I think we're beginning to understand each other.

Scene 2

(Slide of Alice *as a child, riding on her father's back.)*

*(*Alice *lays on the ground, while the* Cowboy *and the* Man *sit huddled around a flask of liquor.)*

Man: Four years old.

Cowboy: Yep.

Man: That's terrible.

Cowboy: I couldn't do a thing.

Man: When Alice was four, she'd walk in to the men's rest room just to get a peek.

Cowboy: So would my—

Man: By six, she knew all the men in my office by name…and size.

Cowboy: No kidding?

Man: They thought it was cute.

Alice: Do you mind?

Man: What?

Alice: It's three in the morning.

Man: So?

ALICE: Shut up.

MAN: Hey. Show some respect for your father.

ALICE: Stop talking about me.

MAN: You're interesting.

COWBOY: We really haven't even scratched the surface. She has some real issues with you.

MAN: Does she?

COWBOY: It's clear to me.

MAN: How's that?

COWBOY: Looking for love. Attention. Genuine affection. But seeking it in men that will never give it to her.

MAN: Huh.

COWBOY: Did you ignore her when she was a child?

ALICE: Yes.

MAN: No.

COWBOY: Did you make her feel she was the most important thing to you?

ALICE: No.

MAN: I drove all over this goddamn country trying to bring her home, didn't I?

COWBOY: Did you listen to her?

ALICE: No.

MAN: Of course I listened to her. She said some funny things as a kid. You should have heard them.

COWBOY: Did you—

MAN: She once asked my mother, point blank—who's got an ass the size of a minivan—if all grandmother's had big butts. Oh, I loved that. My mother didn't, of course.

COWBOY: Of course—

MAN: And, and then one time, when she saw an old broom in my mother-in-law's closet, she asked if she ever rode it. Believe me, if you met my mother-in-law, you'd know this kid was just calling a spade a spade.

ALICE: Dad?

MAN: What?

ALICE: I never said those things.

MAN: Yes you did.

ALICE: How do you know?

MAN: I heard you.

ALICE: How could you?

MAN: With my ears. Jesus.
(To the COWBOY*)*
Is this girl nuts, or what?

ALICE: You weren't there.

MAN: Yes I was.

ALICE: No. You weren't.

MAN: Of course I was.

ALICE: You were not. Mom told you about those things. Grandma told you those things. You weren't there.

MAN: Where was I?

ALICE: Working.

MAN: Oh, now you're gonna throw that in my face, are you?

ALICE: It's true.

MAN: Who paid for that private school? The Ivy League college?

ALICE: Here we go.

MAN: *(To* COWBOY*)* A man works his ass off, sacrifices much of his free time, his leisure time, his own needs and pleasures, to provide for his family, and I have provided WELL for my family. WELL. Believe me. I own a fucking mansion. This girl has got a goddamn silver spoon in her hand, and she's been trying to poke me in the eye with it since she was born.

COWBOY: I see.

MAN: Look at me. Look at my shoes. Covered in dirt and god knows what else out here. And she thinks I don't care about her.

ALICE: You don't.

MAN: See?

ALICE: You're great in crisis, Dad, but the everyday stuff. You suck.

MAN: You think so?

ALICE: Yes.

MAN: And that Rob fellow was Mr Perfect?

ALICE: Let's not talk about him.

MAN: You tell me I'm a worthless father, but you date these worthless men, time and time again, and then conclude you want to kill yourself over them. Tell me where I went wrong.

ALICE: I don't want to talk about it.

COWBOY: Sticky, complicated business, isn't it?

MAN: Sticky indeed.

ALICE: Shut up. Both of you.

MAN: This girl has had nothing but venom for me since the day she could talk—eight months old, complete sentences—

COWBOY: Really?

MAN: Amazing, huh?

COWBOY: Yeah—

MAN: "Fuck you, Dad… Up yours, Dad. You don't care about me. Here's a dime, Daddy, go call someone who gives a shit." So on and so forth. But lathers on all the sweet charm and the gentle kindness for these no good fucks that don't even hold a candle to me. What do you think of that?

COWBOY: Well, seems like a classic example of seeking approval—

MAN: I mean it. Half of these jokers barely even notice she's there. I've watched them. She buys them gifts and cooks goddamn gourmet meals and writes them love poems, and they could give a rat's ass about her. Don't give her the time of day. What do you think of that?

COWBOY: Unfortunate.

(ALICE *stands up.*)

ALICE: Listen, Pops, why don't you just follow my trail right on back to your car and get the fuck out of here. I don't want your help.

MAN: Is that right?

ALICE: It is.

MAN: Then why'd you have Rob call me.

(ALICE *suddenly changes mood.*)

ALICE: He called you?

MAN: Yeah—

ALICE: Worried about me?

MAN: Yes—

ALICE: Really? He called you?

MAN: Yes.

ALICE: When?

MAN: I don't know. Few days ago—

ALICE: What'd he say?

MAN: I don't now—

ALICE: He was worried?

MAN: I guess—

ALICE: What else?

MAN: You were acting strange—

ALICE: Strange?

MAN: Had bought some guns—

ALICE: It's a free country—

MAN: You had a fight—

ALICE: That's an understatement—

MAN: You broke up—

ALICE: And?

MAN: You broke up—

ALICE: Well, well, was he sorry? Did, did he miss me—

MAN: And he thought I should know.

ALICE: Did he want me back?

(MAN *thinks.*)

MAN: No.

ALICE: No?

MAN: No…didn't mention that.

ALICE: Are you sure?

(MAN *thinks.*)

MAN: Positive.

ALICE: Absolutely positive?

MAN: We didn't talk long.

ALICE: Why not?

MAN: It was long distance—

ALICE: Dad—

MAN: What's to say? I don't know the guy—

ALICE: Still. You could have pried.

MAN: I'm here, aren't I?

ALICE: Are you sure he didn't want me back?

MAN: Not to my knowledge.

ALICE: Fucker.

MAN: I never liked him.

ALICE: Who asked you?

MAN: Too damn charming for his own good.

ALICE: He was charming.

COWBOY: Charm is often masking a deep insecurity.

ALICE: Who asked you?

COWBOY: A need for approval.

MAN: Huh.

COWBOY: Masking hidden fears of inadequecies—

ALICE: I hear Western wear is often used to mask a
pain in the ass.

COWBOY: I've never heard that.

ALICE: Look it up.

COWBOY: Where?

ALICE: Stand still while I bend over.

MAN: Alice.

ALICE: Or better yet. Knock me out. You might get
lucky.

MAN: Alice.

ALICE: I hear you like 'em in the dark.

MAN: Alice!

ALICE: What?

MAN: Control yourself.

ALICE: I'm tired of controlling myself.

MAN: Control yourself.

ALICE: Don't you get it—

MAN: I spoiled you.

COWBOY: Actually, I happen to agree on that—

ALICE: Who am I controlling myself for? Huh? You?
Him? Me? Who? What's the fucking point?

MAN: We're going to get it you straightened out—

ALICE: How? You gonna remove my heart?

MAN: I'm sure they've got some kind of instrument—

ALICE: You gonna take out all my hormones?

MAN: Well, I'm sure they got a pill for that—

ALICE: You gonna cut out my clit?

MAN: That's enough of that talk.

ALICE: Are you?

MAN: Of course not.

ALICE: Then you're shit out of luck. There will be no
controlling me, Dad. This is who I am. Tried and true.
Twenty percent Lust. Eighty percent Desire. So if you
don't mind, I'd like to do what I came out here to do.
And I'm sorry if it makes you and mother a little sad
to see me go, and it might look bad in front of your
friends that you couldn't save me and they might
whisper that it was just a matter of time and that I've
always seemed a little odd to them anyway. Who could
disagree? So. I'm gonna get it all over with because the
fact of the matter is, I am BOY CRAZY. BOY CRAZY.
I love men more than I love life itself. And if I can't

have the ones I want, because it appears, survey says, they continue not to want me, I don't want me either. I don't care how many shrinks and pills you toss my way, throw down my throat, they aren't gonna cure this pattern, this dynamic, this history, this injustice. Because it's this very tragic turmoil that I find THRILLING, Dad. Heart-stabbingly wrist slashing suicidely head in the oven gar running in the garage— exhilarating. I'm addicted to the shove away. The push makes me shake. His silence makes me smile. Ignore me, and I'm at your feet. Tell me you don't love me, and I'm your slave. I'm a junkie, Dad. And I'm finally overdosed. If you look closely, you can see the track marks down my arm. It's a trail where I've begged the men to touch me.

MAN: I don't want to hear anymore.

ALICE: One by one. Here and here. And here.

MAN: You're a beautiful girl.

ALICE: Once on my leg— You think I'm beautiful, Dad?

MAN: Yes.

ALICE: Thank you.

MAN: You break me heart, Alice.

ALICE: I'm sorry.

MAN: I want to help.

ALICE: I'm sorry.

MAN: I love you.

ALICE: You say that.

MAN: I do.

ALICE: It's not enough.

MAN: Nothing's enough for you.

ALICE: It's a hunger. I have it.

MAN: It's a waste.

ALICE: Remember the time I ran off with that fry cook?

MAN: I don't want to remember—

ALICE: He didn't speak a word of English, but he looked like an ancient Aztec statue. He was stunning.

MAN: Stunning—

ALICE: He took me down to meet his family in Mexico, and on the way there, we stopped in every village along the way and drank ourselves silly. By the time we got to his parents house, he hated me. You know why?

MAN: I don't want to know, Alice—

ALICE: He hated me because even when I was so drunk I couldn't distinguish my feet from my hands, so wasted, I couldn't speak a word of English either, I could still look him in the eye and see his heart. Closing. Accuse him of not loving me enough. Even when his arms had barely left my side in two weeks, I could tell that I was losing him. The minute I sniffed that out, smelled rejection crossing the border between me and him, I was on him like sweat. Stuck.

MAN: Alice—

ALICE: And he began to hate me.

MAN: You're too much.

ALICE: I'm bigger than life, Dad.

MAN: Well—

ALICE: That's why I can't take it anymore.

MAN: No—

ALICE: Love is too small.

MAN: You underestimate people—

ALICE: Sex, sex is a moment of heaven's expanse, it's eternal light, the taste beyond our bodies and this earth's humble limitations, but then it's back to the miniscule. The tiny pieces that lovers will actually allow each other; finger nails of trust, thimbles of honesty, selfless pleasures on pin heads… The disappointment of clothes—

MAN: Alice—

ALICE: Death is all-consuming, isn't it?

MAN: You're just confused—

ALICE: Big and Complete and Fearless. It will meet me head on. Where men fear to tread, it will be my most Perfect Lover. The Great Endless Orgasm—

MAN: You're confused, Alice! Wrong!

ALICE: No. I just—I want to swallow men, Daddy—

MAN: I know—

ALICE: Whole.

MAN: I know. You exhaust me—

ALICE: I can't help it. I see them and I'm just not satisfied until I've chewed away, soaked them dry and found what's at the bottom of them. "What's inside there, fellow. Let me see You. I want to see all of you, Mister. Open up." And I start digging. And digging. And then once I get to that place, in them, way down there, it's a pit, Dad. It's black and scary and horrible screams echo forth. Loneliness. Gaping despair and old hurt. Cowardice. Lost beauty. Impotence. Fear. Ambition they'll never enjoy. Things I can relate to, I really can. Things I have too. I want to show them that I have those things too… "Let's reveal ourselves together, Boy! What do you say we make dioramas of our chests for each other, huh? Here's my hidden mess, my screaming child—I'll show you mine if you'll show me yours."—

MAN: Your favorite game—

ALICE: But…but…it's always too late… It's already started. The disgust. They've begun to hate me because they didn't want anyone to see that void in there; they don't want anyone to see that. That empty place. Not even themselves, much less a woman. Once I've struck that hole inside them, and I won't stop until I get there, believe me, it's the beginning of saying good-bye. I start crying an hour after I've met each new man because I know the digging and the shadows and the good-bye has just begun.

MAN: You just need to control yourself.

ALICE: "Skate on the surface, girl."

MAN: Lighten up.

ALICE: "Be coy."

MAN: Respect people's privacy.

ALICE: "Just listen and nod."

MAN: Men like to be in charge of things.

ALICE: "Cross you legs and smile."

MAN: A little mystery is good.

ALICE: "Play hard to get".

MAN: Men like to chase a woman a bit.

ALICE: "Don't call him, let him call you."

MAN: They don't want to be emasculated, Alice.

ALICE: "Watch what you say."

MAN: You can't just drill people about things.

ALICE: "Act impressed."

MAN: Control yourself.

ALICE: "Put a sock in it".

COWBOY: Might I suggest something?

ALICE: "Put a sock in it".

MAN: It's getting late. I need my sleep. We got a big day ahead of us tomorrow—

ALICE: I'm not leaving here, Daddy.

MAN: You are.

ALICE: I'm not.

MAN: We'll see about that.

ALICE: This is where I belong.

MAN: You belong where you can get help.

COWBOY: Might I—

ALICE: No—

MAN: Look, Alice, I know there's only so much a father can do. Really. I know that.

ALICE: Daddy—

MAN: Let me finish—

ALICE: I don't want—

MAN: You think you can give your kids everything they're ever gonna need. Everything in the world. All the right toys and schools and decent genetics and enough money to claim their stake in this country. And it takes a whole hell of a lot of money to start at the top of this Great country now. Millions. My dad left me a broken Timex and a pencil. That's it—

ALICE: "And it was chewed."—

MAN: So I made sure my kids had it all. The works. At their disposal. I worked my ass off to give my kids the moon. But still there's only so much, in the end, you can really do as a father. You can't count on <u>Who</u> your kids are gonna be, can you? You can't account for that. *Who* they're gonna be.

ALICE: "Why'd I have to have *girls*?"—

MAN: And what troubles and quirks and neurosis they have inside them, from the get-go, that all the love and money can't change. You can't account for that.

ALICE: "*Girls?*".

MAN: And disease. What if you got cancer? I couldn't control or change that, could I? And you know how that makes me feel, kid? Do you, Alice? …That makes me feel like the most goddamn impotent man on earth. Like I have got nothing to offer as a man in this entire universe. I'm just a useless sack of shit. Poor as dirt, and without an arm or leg to even lean on. A complete stump of a human being. A thud. That's it.

ALICE: I'm not looking for your help, Dad… You're free—

MAN: I am not free! I never will be free with you as my daughter, don't you get it!

ALICE: No!

MAN: We're stuck!

ALICE: No!

MAN: Blood to blood! Seed to stalk! We have the same hungry eyes! Passion! Thirst! I bit into the world and made a man of myself, out of nothing! You are made of the same stuff, girl!—

ALICE: No. I'm not—

MAN: You are your father's daughter! Bold! And I would have killed myself a hundred times just to save you—

ALICE: No—

MAN: You're *my* mess, Alice! You want to see my pit, Alice? Huh? Do you?

ALICE: No.

MAN: I'll take you home and stand you in front of the mirror! We'll stand side by side. You're all that is dark and scary in me. My failure and success and passion and pride. You're my walking wound, sweetheart—

ALICE: I don't want to hear it—

MAN: But I'm not afraid of you, you hear? I'm not. Death may seem a lot easier than growing up, Alice, but it's not. It's just faster.

ALICE: Go. I don't need your guilt-

MAN: It's not guilt, Alice, it's the truth. Fact. Father's honor… Now, we can go home and work this mess out, and we're gonna do it right this time. Side by side. You'll never want to run away again. You'll be calm. Courageous. You'll be just as content as the come—

ALICE: I don't want to be content, Dad. I want to be blissful—

MAN: Or, we can stay here til we freeze to death together, looking like idiots, eating all this cowboy fellow's food—and you know what beans do to me— but I am not going to leave you out here alone.

ALICE: I didn't ask for you to come.

COWBOY: Might I suggest—

ALICE: I've never asked for you to come after me, Dad. Never. Not once.

MAN: But I had to, Alice. Didn't I?

ALICE: For you? Or for me?

MAN: Both of us.

ALICE: Then go home.

COWBOY: Could I offer a small—

MAN: No.

(ALICE *pushes the* MAN.)

ALICE: Go. I don't want you here. I don't want either of you. I don't need male keepers out here, alright? Especially neither of which finds me particularly wonderful at the moment. Both of you are hanging on to me by duty, not by love. So fuck off. Take a ride down the Ponderosa.

(ALICE *pushes the* COWBOY. *Then the* MAN *again.*)

ALICE: Take a hike home, Dad. I would like to be alone.

(The COWBOY *cocks his gun.)*

COWBOY: Let's just get one thing straight. No more cracks about my clothes.

MAN: Sure.

COWBOY: I like the way I look.

MAN: Fine.

COWBOY: I didn't come out here looking for either of your opinions, I came out here to find a little peace, a little reflection, and all I've had from you.
(Looks to ALICE*)*
Is insult and disrespect.

ALICE: You call fucking me without my consent, respect?

MAN: What—

COWBOY: You asked for it.

ALICE: Not like that.

COWBOY: You begged for it.

ALICE: Not like that.

COWBOY: You got what you asked for. And you. *(To the* MAN*)* Coming out here thinking you can save the day. Marching in on my glory.

MAN: What glory?

COWBOY: I can save this bitch on my own. Alright?

ALICE: Hey—

MAN: Listen—

COWBOY: You may think it's real funny, real cute, teasing a man about his choice of outfits, his best uniform, but you can't accuse him of not being able to take care of a girl. Do what's right. Can you? Not being able to watch out for her, make sure she's safe, at all times—

ALICE: You hit me on the head—

COWBOY: YOU ASKED FOR IT!

ALICE: Not like that.

COWBOY: And I am not the type man to walk across the plains and not lend a helping hand to a woman in need—no, a lost and fucked up girl, trying to get a little more attention from her daddy and every other guy that's dumped her because she's such a god-awful spoiled brat. I may hate her guts, but I'm not gonna let her die. I'm not going to give her that pleasure because it's SELFISH and it's STUPID and no one should have to live through that. Alright.
(He holds up the jaw bone.)
I should know!

ALICE: But.

COWBOY: It's cruel. To everyone.

ALICE: You know what?

COWBOY: I don't care.

ALICE: I don't think that's a human bone.

COWBOY: What?

ALICE: I don't.

COWBOY: What?

ALICE: Nope...I think that looks an awful lot like a coyote bone.

COWBOY: No—

ALICE: See, I ran off to Gallup one time and got lost with an Indian Warrior—

MAN: Oh, hell...that was something. Sixteen. She stole a Camero—

ALICE: Firebird—

MAN: From the neighbor kid, took my rifle, eight packs of cigarettes and a fifty dollar bill from my dresser, and her mother's brand new chinchilla coat. I couldn't find her for a month—

ALICE: Like Rain Falls. Wow. He was well hung—

MAN: Alice. Please. I'm too tired to hear that kind of—

ALICE: And we came across a lot of old coyote bones up near his reservation. We slept naked, on dried skins, out under the stars, right beside those bones. They were about that size.

COWBOY: So?

ALICE: Maybe you're full of shit.

(The COWBOY puts the gun in ALICE's face.)

COWBOY: Would I lie about that?

ALICE: You might.

COWBOY: And what good would that do me?

ALICE: Makes you seem mysterious. Dark. Brave.

COWBOY: I don't need the attention. Not like you—

ALICE: Makes it appear that there's more to you than just a rich, bored kid in a country costume, eating trail mix while looking for Himself by way of our nation's national parks... Get a subscription to Ranger Rick. It's a helluva lot cheaper.

COWBOY: I'm gonna blow your fucking brains out.

MAN: Easy, Cowboy.

COWBOY: Walt! My name is Walt!

MAN: Walt—

COWBOY: *(He holds up the bone)* I wouldn't make this up—

ALICE: It did hold my interest. For awhile—

MAN: Short for Walter?

COWBOY: I came to bury it. For good—

MAN: My father's name.

COWBOY: Re—Really?

ALICE: Spooky—

MAN: Sure enough. Good man.

COWBOY: Uh huh. I came to put it to rest—

MAN: A complete failure at everything he ever tried.

COWBOY: Uh huh—

ALICE: But when I looked closer—

MAN: Except alcohol. He was a terrific drunk—

COWBOY: Really—

ALICE: It was too sharp—

MAN: Best in town—

COWBOY: I'm sorry to hear that—

ALICE: To be a child's—

COWBOY: It's all I have—

MAN: Well, hell…what are gonna do. But carry him home on your back and dump in bed next to your mother. Patient woman.

COWBOY: I guess so—

ALICE: But the story—

MAN: Oklahoma folks. The one's that stayed home during the Depression. Not the sharpest tacks in the State, know what I mean?

COWBOY: I guess—

MAN: Thought the term "dust bowl" was just an unkind exaggeration by all the people who made it to California.

COWBOY: Really?

MAN: Ever eaten cats?

COWBOY: No.

MAN: Don't recommend it.

(ALICE *begins to make a move to steal the gun, letting the* MAN *distract the* COWBOY.)

COWBOY: What's it taste like?

MAN: Mice.

COWBOY: Really?

ALICE: Rather compelling—

MAN: Exactly.

COWBOY: Wow.

MAN: Where'd you grow up?

(*Silence*)

COWBOY: New York.

MAN: No kidding?

COWBOY: Manhattan.

ALICE: A brave attempt—

MAN: I love New York. What does your old man do?

(Silence)

COWBOY: Banker.

ALICE: To impress me—

MAN: What's his name?

COWBOY: Al Carter.

MAN: Al Carter? Al Carter? I know Al!

COWBOY: Really?

MAN: Yeah. Tall guy. Loaded.

ALICE: To shock me—

COWBOY: That's him.

MAN: He's big money, Al. Huge.

COWBOY: I suppose.

MAN: How do you like that.

COWBOY: Yeah.

MAN: I heard he had a son.

COWBOY: Yeah?

MAN: Kind of a drifter—

COWBOY: That's my brother—

MAN: Kind of wild. A trouble maker—

COWBOY: My brother—

ALICE: Bedazzle me—

MAN: Al must have given you a pretty little nest egg.

COWBOY: I guess—

MAN: He let you spend it? I hear he's pretty tight—

COWBOY: I bought a ranch.

ALICE: Throw me—

MAN: You don't say?

COWBOY: As far from him as possible.

ALICE: To live.

(ALICE *gets close enough to the gun to grab it when the* COWBOY *pulls it away.*)

COWBOY: Keep your daughter away from me.

MAN: She's just a little playful.

COWBOY: You two make a good team.

MAN: You think so?

ALICE: "Paper Moon"

MAN: Ryan and Tatum O'Neal. Fantastic film—

ALICE: Dad's favorite—

MAN: Wonder what happened to that little Tatum—

COWBOY: But I'm the one with the bullets.

MAN: I see that—

COWBOY: So back off.

MAN: Did your old man teach you to shoot?

COWBOY: No.

MAN: No?

COWBOY: I learned it—

ALICE: From who? Howdy Doody?—

COWBOY: Myself—I'm gonna blow that smart mouth off you in two seconds—

MAN: Easy—

COWBOY: Tell her to shut up.

MAN: I've tried. Believe me.

COWBOY: You better try harder.

MAN: I told you, she's a genius.

ALICE: Daddy—

MAN: Worst curse a kid could have. Knows too much, forgets too little, and has got way too much packed in her little brain when she should've been out just laughing and catching butterflies with the rest of the kids.

ALICE: I did that.

MAN: Never.

ALICE: I did.

MAN: You chased boys instead.

ALICE: Maybe.

MAN: Brought them home roped and tied, and wanted to keep them in a box in your room.

ALICE: What's wrong with that?

MAN: Boys' parents never did understand the details.

ALICE: I put newspaper down.

MAN: I remember feathers. Some kind of nest you built—

ALICE: I planned to feed them.

MAN: Oh sure.

ALICE: And care for them.

MAN: Of course.

ALICE: Kiss them.

(The MAN rolls his eyes.)

ALICE: They were willing.

MAN: They screamed their heads off. I had to pay off some of their parents.

ALICE: Babies.

MAN: Listen, Walt. Why don't you and I strike a deal?

ALICE: No deals, Daddy.

MAN: I'm not going to offer you money because I know you've got plenty.

COWBOY: I'm not ashamed of that—

MAN: I didn't say you were—

COWBOY: I'm just as entitled to that money as—

MAN: Of course you are. I've always insisted Alice work for a living, despite our big wads of dough, but some fathers would rather just hand their kids an easy ride.

ALICE: And look how great I turned out.

COWBOY: It hasn't been an easy ride—

MAN: Of course not. I'm sure your father's very proud of you, Walt.
(Silence)
Now. Why don't we all just cool off. Get some shut eye, and start fresh in the morning. Okay?

COWBOY: I don't trust you.

MAN: Look, son, I'm too tired for games. I've got no weapons on me. I got a wallet full of bills. A set of keys. And a daughter with a sharp tongue. That's it. Oh, and I got blisters on my damn feet from these shoes. I'm too old to stay up late like this, and your threats are getting pretty damn disturbing here, don't you think?
(Silence)

COWBOY: I'm tired too.

MAN: We all are. Lord, you know how far I walked today?

COWBOY: Did you follow the path?

MAN: What path?

ALICE: He has a thing for going the 'right way'. He's on a 'personal journey'.

COWBOY: I don't want to hear another word out of her.

MAN: I'll see what I can do.

COWBOY: And I'm the one that's gonna lead us out of here in the morning. One by one.

MAN: Be my guest.

COWBOY: Tell her to sleep over there. And you sleep there. If either of you tries to touch my gun, I'll use it. I swear, I won't flinch. I'll blow your faces off.

MAN: It's a deal. Alice?

ALICE: What?

MAN: Can you shut up for a few hours? So I can get some sleep?

ALICE: You look awful.

MAN: Well, I'm tired.

ALICE: I don't want you to collapse on me or have a stupid heart attack or a conniption fit or something.

MAN: If you don't shut up, I might.

ALICE: Don't tempt me.

MAN: And if you let this Walt character keep yelling at you all night, pointing that gun around at us, threatening to shoot our faces off, I'm liable to cry.

(ALICE *looks the* COWBOY *and the* MAN *over.*)

MAN: It won't be pretty.

ALICE: I'm only doing it for you sake. Not for his.

MAN: Fine.

ALICE: I really don't like the idea of either one of you here. Spoiling my party. Raining on my death parade.

(*The* MAN *lets out a big sigh.*)

MAN: We can talk about it in the morning.

(ALICE *looks the* COWBOY *and the* MAN *over.*)

ALICE: Fine.

COWBOY: I don't want to hear a word.

ALICE: You might hear a coyote.

MAN: Alice.

ALICE: I—

MAN: Alice.

ALICE: Fine.

MAN: Good night.
(*He lies down.*)

(*The* COWBOY *points the gun, as he slowly lays down.*)

ALICE: Can I say good night?

COWBOY: No.

(ALICE *lays down.*)

Scene 3

(*Slide of* ALICE *in her father's shoes.*)

(ALICE *wakes.*)

(*The* COWBOY *and the* MAN *are still sleeping.*)

(ALICE *stands, quietly steals the* COWBOY's *gun from his hands.*)

(*She backs away from the men, looks around her, and slowly puts the gun in her mouth. She shuts her eyes. She opens eyes and looks down at her father. She quickly removes the gun, remembering she's forgotten something.*)

(ALICE *walks over and leans down to kiss the* MAN—)

ALICE: Good night—

(Upon kissing the MAN, ALICE *feels something is wrong. He's ice cold.)*

ALICE: Daddy?
(She tries to shake him.)
Dad?
(She shakes him.)
Daddy?
(She shakes him again.)
Daddy?
(She lays her head on his chest.)
Please wake up.

(The COWBOY *wakes.)*

ALICE: Daddy? Please. Wake up.

COWBOY: What's the matter—give me my gun?

*(*ALICE *points it at the* COWBOY.*)*

ALICE: Get back. Get away.
(Silence)
Daddy?

COWBOY: What's wrong with him?

*(*ALICE *lays her whole body on the* MAN.*)*

ALICE: Daddy.

COWBOY: What's wrong with him?

ALICE: You killed him.

COWBOY: What? I did not—

ALICE: You killed him. Saying those things to me. About me. He shouldn't have to hear those things. About me.

COWBOY: You killed him.

ALICE: I did not—

COWBOY: Broke his heart.

ALICE: I didn't.

COWBOY: Poor—

ALICE: Fuck you.

COWBOY: Chasing you around at his age.

ALICE: He wanted to do it.

COWBOY: Hiking for miles.

ALICE: He always came.

COWBOY: Worried sick.

ALICE: He always found me.

COWBOY: Tired old man.

ALICE: Always.

COWBOY: Thankless bitch.

ALICE: He loved me.

COWBOY: You killed him—

ALICE: He loved me!

(The COWBOY *backs away.)*

(Silence)

*(*ALICE *lies there crying on the* MAN.*)*

ALICE: He loved me.

(She finally gets up. Gently removes his shoes.)

(The COWBOY *moves toward her.)*

ALICE: Stay there.

*(*ALICE *points the gun at the* COWBOY, *but keeps her eyes on the* MAN.*)*

COWBOY: Where are you going—

ALICE: I said, stay there!
(She moves closer to the COWBOY. *Keeps the gun on him. She kisses his cheek. Backs away)*

Keep the bone story. Coyote or not.

COWBOY: It's not a story.

ALICE: It's a good one.

COWBOY: It's a not a story.

ALICE: You can't save them all.
(She keeps the gun on him.)

COWBOY: Where are you going?

ALICE: None of your business.

COWBOY: It's still dark.

ALICE: I'll follow the stars.

COWBOY: Where?

ALICE: It's a map up there, you know.
(She backs away.)

COWBOY: What, what about your father? Are you just going to leave him here?

(ALICE backs away, the MAN's shoes in her hands.)

(Sound of a gun shot O S)

Scene 4

(Slides of blurred images of ALICE running, at different ages.)

(Sound of crying O S)

(Gun shot)

(Slide of stars)

(Sound of breathing O S)

(Gun shot)

(Slide of the Badlands, sunrise. The road out of the park in the distance)

(Sound of crying O S)

(Gun shot)

(Slide of ALICE as a baby in her father's arms. They are both smiling.)

(Slide of the road out of the Badlands)

(ALICE stands in the middle of the stage, the morning sun in her face. The gun lays on the ground.)

(She holds a handful of dead rabbits in one hand, while the other hand keeps a patient thumb out to hitch hike. The MAN's shoes stand on the ground beside her. They wait for a ride home.)

END OF PLAY